ISBN 978-0-282-42568-5
PIBN 10851497

This book is a reproduction of an important historical work. Forgotten Books uses
state-of-the-art technology to digitally reconstruct the work, preserving the original format
whilst repairing imperfections present in the aged copy. In rare cases, an imperfection in
the original, such as a blemish or missing page, may be replicated in our edition. We do,
however, repair the vast majority of imperfections successfully; any imperfections that
remain are intentionally left to preserve the state of such historical works.

1 MONTH OF
FREE
READING

at

www.ForgottenBooks.com

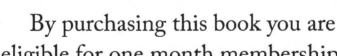

By purchasing this book you are eligible for one month membership to ForgottenBooks.com, giving you unlimited access to our entire collection of over 1,000,000 titles via our web site and mobile apps.

To claim your free month visit:

www.forgottenbooks.com/free851497

FORT
NECESSITY

National Battlefield Site, Pennsylvania

by Frederick Tilberg

NATIONAL PARK SERVICE HISTORICAL HANDBOOK SERIES No. 19
Washington, D. C., 1954
(Revised 1956)

Contents

Lt. Col. George Washington.   From the painting by Charles Willson Peale.   The original is owned by Washington and Lee University and hangs in Lee Chapel, Lexington, Va.

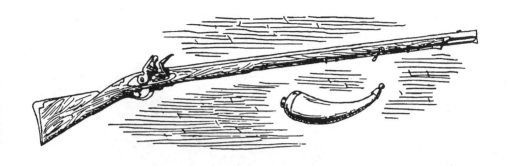

"A volley fired by a young Virginian in the
backwoods of America set the world on fire."

S O HORACE WALPOLE, a contemporary British statesman, described
George Washington's attack on the French at Jumonville Glen
and the resulting action at Fort Necessity. With these two
events occurring on May 28 and July 3, 1754, a war began that was soon
to engulf Great Britain and France on the continent of Europe and
throughout their colonies and was to change radically the balance of
power in America. Here, too, Washington, a lieutenant colonel of
Virginia militia at the age of 22, first commanded troops in action.

Known in America as the French and Indian War and in Europe
as the Seven Years' War, the conflict was destined to establish a new
world order. When formal peace was again restored in 1763, all of
Canada and the whole area east of the Mississippi River, except New
Orleans, became part of the British American domain. "The British
victory," said the historian Francis Parkman, "crippled the commerce
of her rivals, ruined France in two continents, and blighted her as a
colonial power. It gave England control of the seas . . . made her
the first of commercial nations, and prepared that vast colonial system
that has planted new Englands in every quarter of the globe. And
. . . it supplied to the United States the indispensable condition of
their greatness, if not of their national existence."

The clash of imperial colonial policy which brought on the engagement at Fort Necessity produced at the same time one of the first
instances of cooperation among the British colonies in America. Pri-
marily concerned heretofore with their separate interests, colonial gov-
ernors and assemblies were now awakening to the need of working
together for their common interests and for concerted action against
their common enemies.

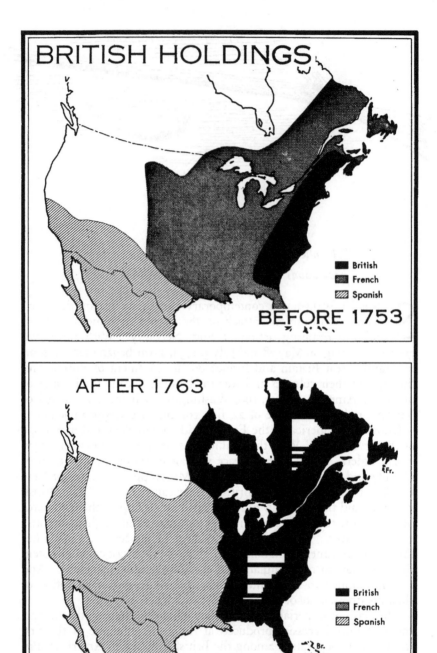

BRITISH HOLDINGS

British
French
Spanish

BEFORE 1753

AFTER 1763

Fr.

British
French
Spanish

Br.

MAP 1

FEB. 1954 NBS-NEC-7004

RIVALRY OF FRANCE AND ENGLAND. In 1749, the Marquis de la Galissonière, Governor General of Canada, sent Pierre-Joseph Celoron de Blainville with about 215 Frenchmen and a force of Indians to take possession of the Ohio Valley for France. The expedition set out from La Chine, Canada, in birchbark canoes and eventually reached the headwaters of the Allegheny River. At Lake Chautauqua, and along the Allegheny, Ohio, and Great Miami Rivers, Blainville posted notices on trees and buried lead plates graven with an inscription asserting that the adjacent lands belonged to the French Crown.

The British likewise had become interested in the fertile lands of the Ohio Valley. Several prominent Englishmen and Virginians, among them Lawrence and Augustine Washington, elder brothers of George, appreciating the potential value of the area and the possibilities for trading posts and settlements, organized the Ohio Company in 1748. The following year, the company obtained from the British Crown a grant of 200,000 acres on both sides of the Ohio between the Monongahela and Great Kanawha Rivers. An additional 300,000 acres was promised if 100 families were settled on the first tract within 7 years. Fearing the encroachment of Pennsylvania settlers, as well as the French, the Ohio Company established a base of operations at Wills Creek, now Cumberland, Md. The company directed the opening of a wagon road to the Monongahela River over a path blazed by Nemacolin, a friendly Delaware Indian. Christopher Gist, explorer and guide, was engaged to locate lands and to determine whether conditions on the extreme frontier were suitable for settlements.

WASHINGTON'S MISSION TO FORT LE BOEUF. The French continued their activities. The new Governor General of Canada, the Marquis Duquesne, sent out an expedition of 1,000 men to build a series of three forts in this region. Forts Presque Isle (near the present city of Erie) and Le Boeuf (in present Waterford) were built in the early summer of 1753. By the time they were completed, however, sickness and the lateness of the season prevented the construction of the third fort. The English trading post at Venango at the junction of French Creek and the Allegheny River (where Franklin is now located) was seized and occupied. Leaving a force to garrison the new posts, the French command returned to Canada for the winter.

News of these developments startled the middle colonies, who were nearest to the zones of friction, and especially alarmed Lt. Gov. Robert Dinwiddie of Virginia. He immediately sent a solemn warning to Legardeur de Saint Pierre, commandant at Fort Le Boeuf, accusing the French of trespassing on the domain of His Majesty, and stating "It is so notoriously known that the Lands on the Ohio River to the

The Marquis Duquesne, Governor General of Canada, 1752–55. Courtesy Public Archives of Canada.

West of the Colony of Virginia belong properly to the Crown of Great Britain." Learning of Dinwiddie's letter, Canada's Governor General Duquesne countered "His claims on the 'Belle Riviere' are a real chimera, for it belongs to us incontestably. Moreover, the King wants it, and that is enough to march ahead." It was clear that the issues were beyond the stage of peaceful settlement.

On October 31, 1753, Governor Dinwiddie appointed one of his adjutants, Maj. George Washington, then 21, to warn the French to withdraw from the Ohio. With Christopher Gist as guide and the Dutch adventurer Jacob Van Braam as interpreter, Washington's party of eight men began the journey through the hazardous frontier country. In the face of winter storms, the little band of men reached the forks of the Ohio (now the site of Pittsburgh) and thence down that river about 17 miles to the Indian village of Logstown. After parleys here with the Indians, Washington continued his journey northward. At Venango, where Celoron had recently dispossessed the Englishman, John Frazier, of his trading post, Washington was received by Capt. Philippe Joincare, the commandant. Joincare referred him to Saint Pierre, the commandant at Fort Le Boeuf. Continuing his march, Washington was now accompanied by the Half King (Tanachariston), a friendly chief of the Senecas, known in this region as the Mingoes, one of the six Iroquois Nations.

The envoy was received at Le Boeuf with marked politeness by the French authorities. In reply to Dinwiddie's demand that the

Robert Dinwiddie, Lieutenant Governor of Virginia. From Douglas Freeman, *George Washington*, Vol. I. Courtesy Charles Scribner's Sons.

French withdraw, the commandant, Legardeur de Saint Pierre, informed Washington that he would hold possession of the Ohio country for France until he received other orders from his superior, the Marquis Duquesne. Meanwhile, the French endeavored to win over the Half King and his Indians. While he accepted a gun and other presents from the French, the Half King nevertheless remained loyal to the English.

Washington returned homeward, after several exciting and dangerous experiences on the way, and delivered the French reply to Dinwiddie at Williamsburg. His mission, however, was not wholly a failure. The young major had taken advantage of the opportunity to learn something of the delicate art of Indian relations, and had gained a firsthand knowledge of French military strength.

THE EXPEDITION AGAINST FORT DUQUESNE. Governor Dinwiddie decided upon a policy of action. In January 1754, under his order, a company of volunteer militia was raised in Virginia to forestall French encroachment. Capt. William Trent was in charge of the small force and, arriving at the forks of the Ohio in February, began to build a log fort. Trent returned to Wills Creek, leaving Ensign Edward Ward and about 40 men to continue building the fort. Before it was half completed, work was ended abruptly. On April 17, some 500 Frenchmen under the command of Capt. Pierre de Contrecoeur appeared suddenly, with artillery, coming down the Allegheny in a

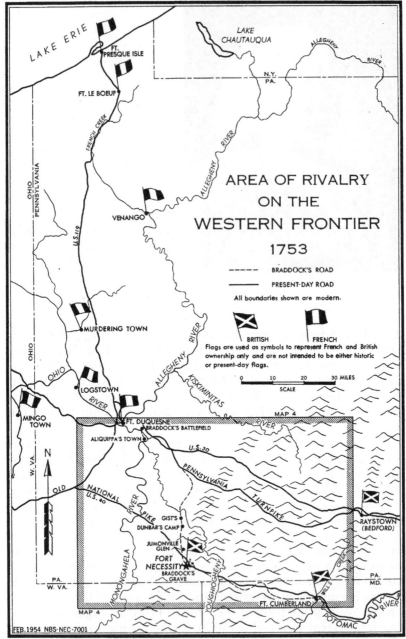

LAKE ERIE

FT. PRESQUE ISLE

LAKE CHAUTAUQUA

N.Y.
PA.

ALLEGHENY RIVER

FT. LE BOEUF

FRENCH CREEK

OHIO
PENNSYLVANIA

ALLEGHENY RIVER

U.S. 119

VENANGO

AREA OF RIVALRY
ON THE
WESTERN FRONTIER
1753

- - - - - BRADDOCK'S ROAD

———— PRESENT-DAY ROAD

All boundaries shown are modern.

BRITISH   FRENCH

Flags are used as symbols to represent French and British
ownership only and are not intended to be either historic
or present-day flags.

0   10   20   30 MILES
SCALE

MURDERING TOWN

ALLEGHENY RIVER

KISKIMINITAS

OHIO

MINGO TOWN

OHIO RIVER

LOGSTOWN

MAP 4

FT. DUQUESNE
BRADDOCK'S BATTLEFIELD
ALIQUIPPA'S TOWN

U.S. 30

W. VA.

N

OLD   NATIONAL   U.S. 40

PENNSYLVANIA   TURNPIKE

RIVER

PIKE

GIST'S
DUNBAR'S CAMP

JUMONVILLE GLEN

FORT NECESSITY
BRADDOCK'S GRAVE

PA.
W. VA.

MONONGAHELA

YOUGHIOGHENY

WILLS CREEK

RAYSTOWN
(BEDFORD)

PA.
MD.

FT. CUMBERLAND

POTOMAC RIVER

MAP 4

FEB. 1954 NBS·NEC·7001

MAP 2

swarm of boats. They compelled Ward to surrender the fort and permitted him to withdraw to the colonies. The French then razed the English fort and proceeded at once to erect a strong fortification which they named Fort Duquesne for the Governor General of Canada. Contrecoeur became commander of the line of forts extending from the Ohio to Presque Isle.

The Virginia Assembly, meanwhile, deemed the situation serious enough to vote money and to raise a force of militia for the campaign. A small regiment of 300 Virginia frontiersmen under Col. Joshua Fry, with George Washington, now a lieutenant colonel, second in command, soon was ready to march to the Ohio to reinforce Ward's party building the fort and to garrison it against anticipated French attack.

The expelled garrison from the fort on the Ohio River, returning homeward, met the reinforcements under Fry and Washington at Wills Creek. Reports from the Ohio brought the alarming news that the French were receiving reinforcements and that the British traders who had ventured into that area were being driven out of the country. The Virginians now took the attitude that the French had committed an act of war. Washington was ordered to proceed to the mouth of Redstone Creek on the Monongahela River, where the Ohio Company had erected a storehouse the preceding year. This point (now the location of Brownsville) was to be the base of operations for the attack on Fort Duquesne. While Fry marched toward Wills Creek, Washington pushed on with a few companies over the Nemacolin Path.

With great difficulty, Washington's force of 60 men succeeded in cutting a road across the mountains. By May 7, the party had reached Little Meadows, having traveled a distance of about 20 miles at an average of 3 miles a day. At the Great Crossing of the Youghiogheny, realizing that the remaining 40 miles would be exceedingly difficult to traverse, Washington sent a detachment down the river by boat to locate a new route. Finding impassable rapids in the river below Turkey Foot (now Confluence), Washington returned to Great Crossing and continued overland westward. On May 24, with the first wheeled vehicle and artillery to cross the Alleghenies, he arrived at Great Meadows, an open swampy vale 50 miles from Wills Creek and 5 miles east of Chestnut Ridge.

The open glade in the forest, with its running brook assuring a water supply, seemed an ideal campsite and a place from which to reconnoiter the country. Learning from the Half King that a strong detachment of French and Indians was on the march from Fort Duquesne, Washington took immediate steps to fortify the position and "placed troops behind two natural Entrenchments and had our wagons put there also." As the work of fortifying the place progressed, Washington reported to Governor Dinwiddie "We have, with Nature's assistance,

Capt. Louis Coulon de Villiers.
Courtesy Pennsylvania Historical and
Museum Commission.

made a good Intrenchment, and by clearing ye Bushes out of these
Meadows, prepar'd a charming field for an Encounter." The natural
entrenchments to which Washington referred were apparently the
banks of Great Meadows Run and Indian Run where they form a
juncture. Although the valley was nearly all marshland, Washington
believed it had military advantages.

THE JUMONVILLE INCIDENT. Events now moved speedily. In the evening of May 27, a runner from the Half King arrived at Great Meadows
with the news that the hiding place of a body of French had been discovered on Chestnut Ridge, 5 miles westward. The Half King had
discovered the trail of two men and had followed it to a deep ravine in
the forest. Fearing that the French were about to attack him, Washington determined at once to dispose of this threat. He left a strong
guard to protect the fort and its stores of ammunition from a surprise
attack and set out with about 40 men in a night "as dark as pitch, along
a path scarce broad enough for one man."

Stumbling along the mountain path in the inky darkness of the
forest and in a heavy rain, frequently losing their way, the party at
dawn reached the Indian camp at Half King's Rocks on the crest of
Chestnut Ridge. Here, Washington and the Half King decided to
attack the French in their hideout at once. Indian scouts led the
way 2 miles northward. The party was soon in the presence of the
enemy who were encamped in a secret glen sheltered by a 30-foot ledge

Washington answered the accusation pointedly in his letter to Governor Dinwiddie in which he stated that ". . . instead of coming as an Embassador, publicly, and in an open manner, they came secretly, and sought after the most hidden retreats . . . encamped there and remained hidden for whole days together, at a distance of not more than five miles from us; they sent spies to reconnoiter our camp . . ."

Half King's Rocks on Chestnut Ridge, where Washington and the Half King planned the attack on Jumonville.

Jumonville Glen.

Responding to the allegation that the French party, when attacked, was on a mission of peace, Washington wrote "They say they called us as soon as they had discovered us; which is an absolute falsehood for I was then marching at the head of the company going toward them and can positively affirm that, when they saw us, they ran to their arms, without calling; as I must have heard them had they so done." Duquesne, on hearing of Jumonville's death, branded it assassination and wrote Contrecoeur that if the English were marching toward Fort Duquesne "with an open show of force, as you have been informed, the break is definite and you will overlook nothing in repelling force with force."

The outcome of the action on Chestnut Ridge was decisive. Washington realized, however, that a strong enemy force might soon fall upon him. Aware of this peril and anticipating French reprisals, he sent a message to Colonel Fry at Wills Creek for reinforcements. The returning messenger informed Washington that Fry had been fatally injured in a fall from his horse, and that the command had devolved upon Col. James Innes, who had recently arrived with his regiment of North Carolina troops. Two New York companies were still at Alexandria, Va., when the French fell upon Washington at Fort Necessity and did not reach Wills Creek until the remnants of Washington's broken little force were returning to the shelter of that fort. Colonel Washington now was given command of the Virginia regiment.

BUILDING THE STOCKADE. While awaiting the arrival of support before making the next move toward Redstone Creek, it became clear to Washington that the small fortifications at Great Meadows needed strengthening if he was to hold his position against a strong attack. Taking advantage of the brief respite, the men were put to work enlarging and strengthening the fort. From his camp at Great Meadows, the young colonel noted in periodic communications the progress of fort construction.

Writing to Governor Dinwiddie of Virginia on May 29, the day after the Jumonville incident, Washington stated "we have already begun a Palisado'd Fort, and hope we can have it up tomorrow . . ."

Washington informed his brother, Augustine, on May 31 "We expect every hour to be attacked by a superior force, but, if they forbear one day longer, we shall be prepared for them. We have already got entrenchments, and are about a pallisado which I hope will be finished today. . . ."

On June 1, Washington noted in his Journal "we are finishing our Fort." Two days later, he again wrote Governor Dinwiddie informing him "We have just finished a small palisado'd fort, in which, with my small numbers, I shall not fear the attack of 500 men."

The remainder of the Virginia regiment, about 200 men, arrived June 9 from Wills Creek under Lt. Col. George Muse. Upon the arrival of these reinforcements, Washington on June 12 took additional measures of preparedness against attack by guarding against "all casualties that might happen to the camp, and ordered Col. Muse to repair into the fort, and erect the small swivels [cannon] for the de fense of the place . . ." On the same day, apparently with reference to his plan of continuing the opening of a road to Redstone Creek, Washington noted in his diary that he ". . . gave orders to Col. Muse, to put away all our baggage and ammunition, and to place them in the Fort, and to set a good guard there till my return." The possible urgent use to be made of the little fort at Great Meadows was indicated in the report of Governor Dinwiddie to the Lords of Trade, dated June 18, in which he stated "our Forces have erected a Stockade Fort near the Monongahela for a retreat on occasion. . . ."

PREPARATIONS FOR BATTLE. Governor Dinwiddie realized that in directing an expedition into a wilderness region a strong force of Indians was important for the kind of warfare typical of the frontier. For this support, he turned to the Catawbas and Cherokees of South Carolina. After extended negotiations, in which he had ignored the assistance offered by Gov. James Glen of that colony, Dinwiddie failed utterly.

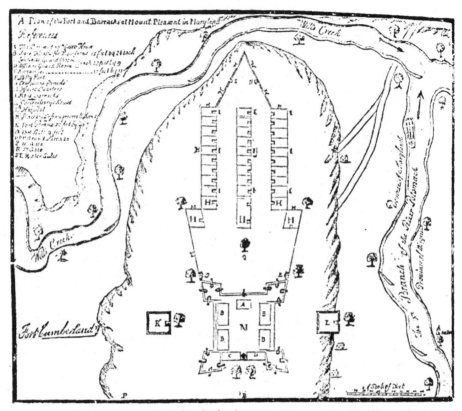

Fort Cumberland, 1755. From Lowdermilk, *History of Cumberland, Maryland.*

The loss of this alliance, coupled with the defection of the Shawnee and Delaware tribes soon to occur, was to leave Washington without a single Indian ally in the action at Fort Necessity. Even the Half King, who had long been friendly to the English, now spoke of Washington as "a good-natured man but [who] had no experience" and that "he lay at one place from one full moon to the other and made no fortifications at all, but that little thing upon the Meadow, where he thought the French would come up to him in open field."

The South Carolina Independent Company of regular troops, commanded by Capt. James Mackay, arrived on June 12, but almost immediately difficulties arose over the difference in the rank between Mackay, a regular who held his commission from the King, and Washington, an officer of the militia. Mackay refused to take orders from Washington and then established a separate camp. He also refused to permit his men to work, without additional compensation, on the proposed road to Redstone. In spite of the trouble within his own force, and with the ominous reports that both the Shawnee and Delaware Indians had definitely joined the French, Washington nevertheless decided to press forward with Redstone as his objective.

Leaving the South Carolina regulars at Great Meadows, Washington, on June 16, ordered the Virginia regiment, with nine swivel guns, to move westward over the rugged mountain paths. Upon reaching Gist's Plantation (now Mount Braddock) on June 18, the regiment encountered a band of Mingo, Shawnee, and Delaware Indians. Washington and the Half King, after a long conference, failed to persuade the Indians to hold to the English alliance, and Washington pushed on toward Redstone. On June 28, when the Virginia force, still engaged in clearing the road, was hardly 8 miles from Redstone, Washington learned that a large force of French and Indians was advancing from Fort Duquesne. It was first agreed, in a council of war, to build sufficient entrenchments to make a stand against the French. Captain Mackay and his regulars from Fort Necessity arrived hurriedly on June 29, and, after a second council, it was decided to give way in the face of the strong foe and to withdraw to Great Meadows.

Having lost heavily in horses and wagons in the advance to Gist's Plantation, the return trip over the mountain with baggage and swivels was accomplished only after men and horses alike were completely exhausted. On July 1, after a continuous march, they reached Great Meadows. Many of the men were ill and fatigued. Faced with the danger of being overtaken by the enemy on the march, Washington decided to make a stand at the little stockade. Only a few days earlier he had referred to it, for the first time, as Fort Necessity.

In the meantime, at Fort Duquesne the rumor that the English with a force of nearly 5,000 troops were advancing westward had impelled Governor General Duquesne to take measures for the protection of the French fort at the forks of the Ohio. News of Jumonville's death had been dispatched quickly from Fort Duquesne to Montreal. Capt. Louis Coulon de Villiers, brother of Jumonville and an experienced soldier, was commissioned to organize a band of Indians and to proceed to Fort Duquesne. Arriving there on June 26, Villiers found that Contrecoeur, the commandant of the fort, had already formed a detachment of 600 French and about 100 Indians under Chevalier le Mercier to march against Washington. Claiming seniority for the command and requesting the opportunity of avenging the death of his brother, Jumonville, Villiers was given charge of the expedition.

Villiers left Fort Duquesne on June 28, and proceeded to the junction of the Monongahela River and Redstone Creek. Leaving a guard here over his boats and supplies, he began on July 1 the march over the hilly country. Soon the party came upon the uncompleted road which had been abandoned a few days earlier by the English. The force

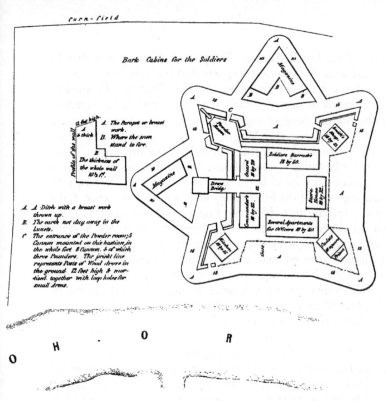

Sketch of Fort Duquesne made by Robert Stobo while a hostage after the Battle of Fort Necessity. From Sargeant, *History of an Expedition Against Fort Duquesne.*

moved slowly and cautiously on July 2 and encamped overnight at Gist's Planatation. At daybreak, July 3, the French again moved forward, in a heavy rain, over the recently built road. Pressing through the drenched forest on the mountainside, pausing briefly at the spot where his brother had been killed and where several bodies still lay exposed, Villiers was soon in the vicinity of the English encampment.

THE FRENCH STRIKE FORT NECESSITY. Great Meadows was a broad valley through which flowed a small, shallow stream. It was largely marshland with a heavy growth of tall grass and bushes. On either side of the swale the land rose gradually to ranges of hills. On the southern hill, woodland covered the crest and the slope to a point within 300 yards on the southwest and about 60 yards on the southeast. North of the valley, woodland extended to a line within 250 yards of the creek. It was at the junction of Great Meadows Run and Indian Run, which approaches from the south, that Washington's fort and stockade had been built.

On July 2, the works had been strengthened, and Mackay's men had constructed entrenchments on the exposed southern side of the stockade in order to broaden the defense position, while the Virginians built rifle pits and embankments near the palisades. In the brief time left to Washington for making battle preparations, he had tried to make "the best Defense their small Numbers w'd admit of, by throwing up a small Intrenchm't, which they had not Time to Compleat. . . ."

Cautiously advancing in mid-forenoon along the Nemacolin Path, under cover of the wooded hills southwest of the fort, Villiers' troops were startled by the firing of a musket. It was one of Washington's sentinels who had given a warning signal that the enemy had been sighted. Within a few minutes, Villiers' men were seen at the edge of the forest.

Unacquainted with the locality, the French at first approached with their flank toward the fort and were fired upon by the swivel guns. "Almost at the same time," Villiers relates, "I noticed the English who were coming toward us in battle array on the right. The savages as well as ourselves shouted the battle cry, and we advanced toward them, but they did not give us time to shoot before they retreated to an entrenchment which belonged to their fort. Then we used all our efforts to surround the fort."

Washington apparently planned at the start to fight a defensive action. His force, now consisting of barely 400 troops, was considerably weakened by the illness of nearly 100 of his men. Part of his

Great Meadows and Fort Necessity from the southwest, the direction from which the French first approached the fort.

force, therefore, was placed in the open ground in front of the entrenchments and, ignoring the first fire of the French, awaited attack in their positions. The French commander failed to draw Washington's men from their stand in front of the entrenchments, and the French force then shifted to the right where "they advanced irregularly within 60 yards of our Forces, and y'n [then] made a second discharge."

Washington, observing that the French did not intend to attack his men in the open field, now ordered them to withdraw to their trenches and reserve their fire until the expected attack upon these defenses. Finding that the French still would not make an attempt against his men in the trenches, Washington ordered them to fire. "We continued this unequal Fight," he relates, "with an Enemy sheltered behind the Trees, ourselves without Shelter, in Trenches full of Water, in a settled Rain, and the Enemy galling us on all Sides incessantly from the Woods, till 8 o'Clock at Night. . . ." At the start of the battle, declared John B. W. Shaw, a member of the Virginia regiment, as the Indians ventured forth from the cover of the trees, Washington ordered his men to fire and at the same time two swivel guns were discharged, the combined volleys killing many of the Indians. "After this," he states, "Neither French nor Indians appeared any more but kept behind Trees firing at our Men the best part of the Day, as our People did at them."

Mercier suggested in the evening that Villiers "pen up the English in their fort during the night and prevent their coming out at all." At about 8 o'clock, however, the French leader, having strengthened his own positions, called to the English that he was willing to negotiate. "We had endured rain all day long and the detachment was very tired," Villiers later noted in his journal. Since the savages "were making known that their departure was set for the next day, and since it was reported that drum-beating and cannon shot could be heard in the distance. . . .", the French commander apparently decided to take the initiative in requesting a cessation of hostilities.

On hearing the French commander call for a truce, Washington was at first hesitant, stating at a later time ". . . we looked upon this offer to parley as an artifice to get into and examine our trenches and refused on this account until they desired an officer might be sent to them, and gave their parole for his safe return. . . ." Upon being assured by this pledge of safety, however, Washington agreed to send two officers, Jacob Van Braam and William Peyronie, to see Villiers. At the meeting in the open meadow between the lines, Villiers informed Van Braam and Peyronie that the French desired to avoid war and stated that their only mission was to avenge the death of his brother Jumonville and to compel English settlers to vacate lands claimed by the French Crown.

In the terms of capitulation handed to Van Braam, Washington

Facsimile of first page and signatures of the *Articles of Capitulation at Fort Necessity.* Courtesy Department of Civil Statutes and of Archives, Superior Court, Montreal, Canada.

Maj. Gen. Edward Braddock, commander of the second expedition against Fort Duquesne.

was permitted to return to his own country with his entire force, except two captains, Robert Stobo and Van Braam, who would be held as hostages for the safe return of French prisoners captured in the action on Chestnut Ridge. Of the equipment, only the cannon were taken from them. Although Governor General Duquesne had consistently maintained that the English had never held a proper claim to lands west of the mountains, Villiers inserted a clause stating that the English were to agree not to construct any defense work west of the mountain range for the period of a year.

This was the substance of the articles of capitulation brought to the fort by Van Braam and examined by Washington. Capt. Adam Stephen later described vividly the manner in which the terms were received. Referring to Van Braam's report on the articles, he wrote: "It rained so heavily that he could not give us a written Translation of them; we could scarcely keep the Candle light to read them; they were wrote in a bad Hand, on wet and blotted Paper so that no person could read them but Van Braam who had heard them from the mouth of the French Officer. . . ." The articles which Washington unwittingly signed referred to Jumonville's death as an assassination. The combination of poor light and Van Braam's meager knowledge of French led him to translate the word orally as "death". Washington was greatly mortified when the error was discovered as the terms were widely circulated in Europe and it was made to appear that he had admitted an assassination. If he had received an accurate translation, he certainly would not have signed it. Every officer present, according to Captain Stephen, was willing to declare that "there was no such word as Assassination mentioned; the Terms expressed to us were 'the death of Jumonville.' "

The capitulation arranged, Washington's survivors prepared to leave, early on July 4, a field on which his little force had fought the strong detachment of French and Indians on equal terms and under trying conditions. Relating that his own losses were 30 killed and 70 wounded, he estimated that 300 of the French and Indian force were killed and many more wounded as the enemy were "busy all Night in burying their Dead, and many yet remained the next Day." Villiers reported a loss of only 20, but another participant, Varin, listed them as 72.

The English force was soon on the homeward journey. The horses and cattle had been killed. The men who were able had to carry the sick and wounded. Harassed by the Indians on the march, they finally reached the base at Wills Creek 50 miles away. As the English band started on its way, Villiers' force "demolished their fort, and M. le Mercier had their cannons broken up . . ." a statement which is partially corroborated by that of Colonel Innes at Wills Creek, which notes that "after the capitulation the French demolished the works."

The Duke of Cumberland. From Cunningham, *Lives of Eminent Englishmen.*

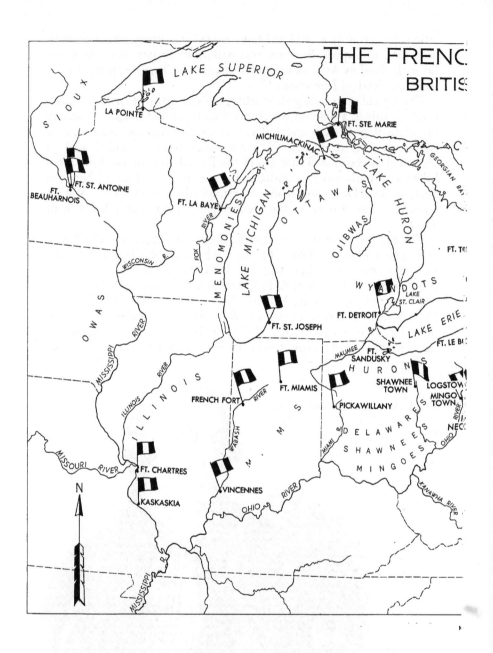

THE FRENC
BRITIS

LAKE SUPERIOR

SIOUX

LA POINTE

FT. STE. MARIE

MICHILIMACKINAC

FT. ST. ANTOINE

FT.
BEAUHARNOIS

FT. LA BAYE

GEORGIAN BAY

C

LAKE HURON

OTTAWAS

OJIBWAS

FT. T(

MENOMONIES

LAKE MICHIGAN

FOX RIVER

WISCONSIN R.

OWAS

WISCONSIN RIVER

MISSISSIPPI RIVER

ILLINOIS RIVER

WYANDOTS

LAKE
ST. CLAIR

FT. DETROIT

LAKE ERIE

FT. LE B(

FT. ST. JOSEPH

MAUMEE R.

FT.
SANDUSKY

FT. MIAMIS

HURONS

SHAWNEE
TOWN

LOGSTOW

PICKAWILLANY

MINGO
TOWN

ILLINOIS

MIAMI R.

DELAWARES

SHAWNEES

NEC(

FRENCH FORT

WABASH R.

MINGOES

S

MISSOURI RIVER

FT. CHARTRES

N

KASKASKIA

VINCENNES

OHIO RIVER

KANAWHA RIVER

OHIO

MISSISSIPPI RIVER

20

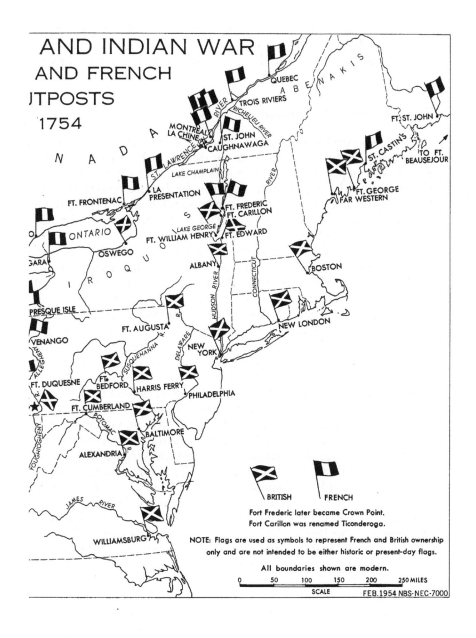

AND INDIAN WAR
AND FRENCH
JTPOSTS
1754

QUEBEC
A B E N A K I S
TROIS RIVIERS
RICHELIEU RIVER
RIVER
FT. ST. JOHN
MONTREAL
LA CHINE
ST. JOHN
CAUGHNAWAGA
ST. CASTIN'S
TO FT.
BEAUSEJOUR
N A D A
ST. LAWRENCE RIVER
LAKE CHAMPLAIN
RIVER
FT. GEORGE
FAR WESTERN
FT. FRONTENAC
LA
PRESENTATION
S
FT. FREDERIC
FT. CARILLON
ONTARIO
LAKE GEORGE
FT. WILLIAM HENRY
FT. EDWARD
OSWEGO
Q
CONNECTICUT
ALBANY
BOSTON
GARA
R O Q U
HUDSON RIVER
PRESQUE ISLE
NEW LONDON
FT. AUGUSTA
R.
VENANGO
SUSQUEHANNA
DELAWARE R.
NEW
YORK
ALLEGHENY
FT. DUQUESNE
FT.
BEDFORD
HARRIS FERRY
PHILADELPHIA
FT. CUMBERLAND
POTOMAC
BALTIMORE
YOUGHIOGHENY
ALEXANDRIA
JAMES RIVER
WILLIAMSBURG

BRITISH   FRENCH

Fort Frederic later became Crown Point.
Fort Carillon was renamed Ticonderoga.

NOTE: Flags are used as symbols to represent French and British ownership
only and are not intended to be either historic or present-day flags.

All boundaries shown are modern.
0   50   100   150   200   250 MILES
SCALE
FEB. 1954 NBS-NEC-7000

Villiers, having completed his mission of driving the English back across the Alleghenies, retraced his path to Redstone and thence by way of the Monongahela to Fort Duquesne which he reached on July 7.

The Braddock Expedition

THE BRITISH AGAIN CHALLENGE THE FRENCH. By the articles of capitulation signed on July 4, 1754, after the action at Fort Necessity, the French now hoped that further conflict in the trans-Allegheny region would be ended. The British, however, far from accepting the unfavorable outcome of that battle as a conclusive test of their strength on the frontier, soon began preparations to challenge again the French power west of the Alleghenies.

The renewed effort to drive the French from the Ohio, however, was not to be a Colonial undertaking. Governor Dinwiddie, attributing the defeat at Fort Necessity to lack of knowledge of French and Indian reinforcements at Fort Duquesne and to the indifference of certain colonies, particularly New York, in supporting the expedition against Fort Duquesne, now began preparation for a new campaign. On July 20, he ordered the enlargement of the post at Wills Creek. A log fort and a storage magazine, capable of holding provisions for 1,200 to 1,400 men over a 6-month period, were built.

With this greatly strengthened establishment, he planned to send some 900 men and 6 swivel guns under Colonel Innes across the Alleghenies in an effort to capture the French fort on the Ohio. The refusal of the officers of the Independent Companies of New York and South Carolina and the mutinous conduct of the Virginia troops compelled Dinwiddie to abandon his plan. The failure of support in his expedition against Fort Duquesne and the lack of Colonial cooperation reflected in the Albany Congress of 1754 led him to believe that only with aid from England could a Colonial force successfully deal with the French. The British Government, therefore, prepared an elaborate plan of attack. Four expeditions were projected against the French strongholds at Fort Duquesne, Fort Niagara, Fort St. Frederic (Crown Point), and Fort Beausejour, with the main thrust directed against Fort Duquesne.

The Duke of Cumberland, Captain General of the British Army and soldier son of the King (George II), now took the initiative in promoting the British campaign against the French. He appointed Maj. Gen. Edward Braddock, an officer of 45 years' service and a veteran of the Coldstream Guards, to be in command of the Fort Duquesne expedition as well as of all British troops in America. With the 44th regiment under Sir Peter Halkett and the 48th under Col. Thomas Dunbar, augmented by Colonials mainly from Virginia and Maryland,

Braddock had assembled a formidable force. Lt. Col. George Washington accepted a place on Braddock's staff as one of the general's three aides-de-camp.

THE ADVANCE OF BRADDOCK'S FORCE. Braddock had arrived at Hampton Roads on February 19 and held a conference with Governor Dinwiddie at Williamsburg concerning the attitude of many of the colonies toward the proposed expedition. Concerned largely during the early spring in negotiations at Williamsburg and Alexandria for detachments of colonial militia and in assembling wagons and horses, he finally arrived at Wills Creek on May 10. During the winter of 1754–55, the trading fort at this place had been transformed into a military establishment named Fort Mt. Pleasant and renamed Fort Cumberland. Here, soon after his arrival, Braddock assembled an army of 2,150 men, a unit of artillery, 500 baggage horses, and 150 Pennsylvania wagons provided through the efforts of Benjamin Franklin. Included in the army were contingents of Colonial troops from Virginia, New York, South Carolina, and Maryland. A company of North Carolina men was on the march to join Braddock. Anticipating the difficulties which would be found in crossing rivers, Braddock had obtained from the British Admiral Keppel a force of 30 sailors to devise means of transporting the army.

By the end of the first week of June, the army was well on its march from Fort Cumberland. Scouts out in front and on the flanks guarded against a surprise attack, while axmen cleared the road to a width of 12 feet for the artillery and baggage wagons. The road-building party consisted of Poulson's Virginia carpenters who, under direction of the engineers, cut trees, built bridges, and performed general duties.

Braddock's advance to Little Meadows was slow. Here, on the advice of Washington, he decided to select 1,300 men and to push forward rapidly. Colonel Dunbar, with the remaining 850 men, the heavy baggage, stores, and the artillery was to advance by slower marches. Two 6-pounders, four 12-pounders, four 8-inch howitzers, and three Coehorn mortars were attached to the leading unit. To cross the mountains each howitzer required a 9-horse team and each 12-pounder cannon, a 7-horse team. The convoy consisted of 30 wagons. Rations for 30 days were carried by 400 pack horses, and 100 spare horses accompanied the column. As part of the food supply the expedition brought with it a large herd of cattle. On June 18, with everything in readiness, 400 men, under the command of Lt. Col. Thomas Gage, moved forward with axes to blaze the way.

The advance detachment thus was decreased by nearly one-half and the extent of the carriages, on the march from Little Meadows, "was very seldom above half a mile . . . and encampments [were] but

Lt. Col. Thomas Gage, commander of the advance unit of Braddock's Army. Courtesy The Commonwealth of Massachusetts.

three hundred yards from the front to the rear. . . ." When the column encamped, it included Gage's advance party, the whole encampment being encircled by a chain of sentries. A member of the expedition noted that on June 25, "we passed the Great Meadows, and encamped about two miles on the other side . . . about a quarter of a mile from this camp, we were obliged to let our carriages down a hill with tackles, which made it later than usual before we got to our ground." Soon Chestnut Ridge, the last great obstacle, was passed, and the army, observing every precaution, pushed on toward Fort Duquesne. As the force approached Turtle Creek on July 8, the commanding officer was unusually apprehensive of danger from hills on his flank and placed strong detachments on these eminences to protect the flanks of the army. On the fateful next day, July 9, Braddock moved forward cautiously.

THE FRENCH PREPARE FOR ACTION. Governor General Duquesne had learned of the overall campaign plans of the British, and he likewise knew that Braddock's two regiments had sailed from Britain. In a countermove, the French Government prepared to send a strong contingent of its best troops to defend French strongholds in the New World. It soon became apparent, however, that the French force would not reach Quebec before the British troops had landed in Virginia and were well on the way toward the Ohio.

Thus, as the crisis for the French at Fort Duquesne approached, the garrison consisted of hardly more than 1,000 Frenchmen and Indians, the latter including small parties from many tribes of the Ohio and Great Lakes country, and the Shawnee, a strong nation, which had now turned against the English. The pressure brought by the British against Fort Beausejour in Nova Scotia, Fort St. Frederic at Crown Point, and at Forts Niagara and Frontenac forced the new Governor General, the Marquis de Vaudreil, who arrived in Quebec on June 26, to divide his forces for the defense of these points. Contrecoeur's command at Fort Duquesne was thus assigned to man its own defenses against Braddock's powerful army.

On July 8, the French at Fort Duquesne were thrown into great confusion by reports from scouts that Braddock's army was just beyond the Monongahela. Contrecoeur, upon the suggestion of either Capt. Lienard de Beaujeu or Capt. Jean-Daniel Dumas, resolved to meet the enemy on the march and to ambush them. The crossing of the Monongahela, 8 miles away, appeared to offer the best conditions for a surprise attack. Early on the morning of July 9, final preparations were hurriedly made, and, with Beaujeu in command, the party of 250 French and 650 Indians, many of whom had drifted off only to return as the fight began, started over the well-beaten path toward Turtle Creek.

THE BATTLE ON THE MONONGAHELA. It was close to 1 o'clock when Braddock crossed the Monongahela and started beyond. Suddenly, the band of French appeared directly ahead. Beaujeu turned and waved his hat to those behind him. Instantly, the war cry was raised. Indians swarmed through the forest to the right and left of the British advance guard. Almost at the first exchange of shots, as Beaujeu fell mortally wounded, many of the Canadians fled from the field. The regular French officers under Captain Dumas, now in command, and Charles Langlade, leader of the Indians, rallied the warriors who poured a deadly fire from behind trees and rocks in two deep ravines. Especially destructive was the fire of the Indians from a small hill on the right of the British. Gage's men, in the vanguard, fell back upon the main body, resulting in increased confusion. Apparently dazed by the sudden and withering attack, the British fired aimlessly into the woods, often shooting down their own Colonial comrades who had chosen to fight Indian fashion from the cover of trees.

As the firing continued, Braddock rode forward. In the midst of the milling mass of troops around him, he apparently sought, as the only way out, to move on to the open country ahead. But every attempt to restore formation and move forward was cut short by the fire of the enemy. Five horses were shot from under General Braddock as he rode among his men trying to restore order. At last he fell, mortally wounded, shot through the arm into the lungs, just after he

Sir Peter Halkett. From Parkman, *Montcalm and Wolfe.*

had ordered a retreat.   In little more than 2 hours the battle was over, the army scattered, with most of its officers either dead or wounded.

The British had suffered a catastrophe.   Of the 1,373 privates and noncommissioned officers, 914 were killed or wounded; of 86 officers, 63 were casualties.   The French loss included only 3 officers killed and 4 wounded; among the privates, 4 French and 5 Canadians were casualties, while 27 Indians were killed or wounded.

All night long and throughout the next day the remnants of Braddock's army fled without order back over the road toward Dunbar's Camp.   At Gist's Plantation they were met by wagons bearing provisions sent by Dunbar who had heard of the disaster from fugitives. The panic did not end with the arrival of the stragglers at Dunbar's Camp.   Wild disorder prevailed in the camp as Dunbar's men, fearful that the French and Indians would suddenly fall upon them, began wanton destruction of arms and ammunition.   In a frenzied attempt to make sure that his equipment and supplies did not fall into French hands, Dunbar destroyed four 12-pounder cannon; 324 rounds of canister were broken and shattered; more than 3,000 cannon balls and shells were buried; and 16,200 pounds of powder were dumped into a spring.   Even 4 years after the incident, Col. James Burd, while passing Dunbar's Camp, "saw vast quantities of cannonball, musket bullets, broken shells, and an immense destruction of powder. wagons, etc."

On July 13, the entire body began the retreat to Fort Cumberland. Toiling down the mountainside, they reached Old Orchard Camp. Here, late in the evening, the mortally wounded Braddock died.   Early

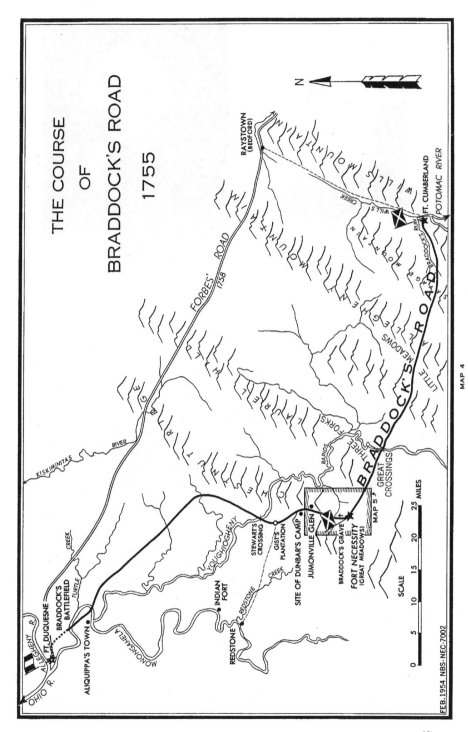

THE COURSE

OF

BRADDOCK'S ROAD

1755

N

RAYSTOWN
(BEDFORD)

ALLEGHENY MOUNTAIN

FORBES' ROAD
1758

FT. CUMBERLAND
POTOMAC RIVER

WILLS CREEK

BRADDOCKS RUN

CHESTNUT RIDGE

LITTLE MEADOWS

BRADDOCK'S ROAD

LAUREL HILL

KISKIMINITAS RIVER

CREEK

TURTLE CREEK

FT. DUQUESNE
BRADDOCK'S BATTLEFIELD

ALLEGHENY R.

OHIO R.

ALIQUIPPA'S TOWN

MONONGAHELA

INDIAN FORT

REDSTONE

REDSTONE CREEK

YOUGHIOGHENY

STEWART'S CROSSING

GIST'S PLANTATION

SITE OF DUNBAR'S CAMP

JUMONVILLE GLEN

BRADDOCK'S GRAVE

FORT NECESSITY
(GREAT MEADOWS)

RAPIDS

THREE FORKS

GREAT CROSSINGS

MAP 5

SCALE
0   5   10   15   20   25   MILES

FEB.1954 NBS·NEC-7002

MAP 4

27

Capt. Lienard de Beaujeu. From
*Pennsylvania Magazine of History and
Biography.*

Capt. Jean-Daniel Dumas. Courtesy Public Archives of Canada.

the following morning, as Washington read the Anglican service, the British general was buried in the middle of the road. Soon, the entire army passed over the grave, effacing all signs which might lead prowling Indians to the place. Three days later, the remnants of the ruined army reached the shelter of Fort Cumberland.

The French victory was rendered possible almost entirely by the powerful bands of Indians. The triumph in the Ohio country of the French and their Indian allies now seemed complete. Not the least of the consequences of this calamitous defeat was the sporadic outbreak of Indian warfare which ravaged the now unprotected English frontier settlements with harrowing and tragic violence. It was not until 1758 that a second and successful campaign finally relieved the Pennsylvania, Maryland, and Virginia frontier from Indian raids. In that year, Gen. John Forbes captured Fort Duquesne, the stronghold of the French in the Ohio Valley, and named the strengthened outpost Fort Pitt, in honor of William Pitt, the Prime Minister whose vigorous prosecution of the war had made victory possible.

Surveys and Excavations of Fort Necessity

In the two centuries that have elapsed since Washington's capitulation and the subsequent destruction of Fort Necessity by Villiers, several attempts have been made to fix the exact location of the fort and to define its construction in detail. Destruction of the stockade

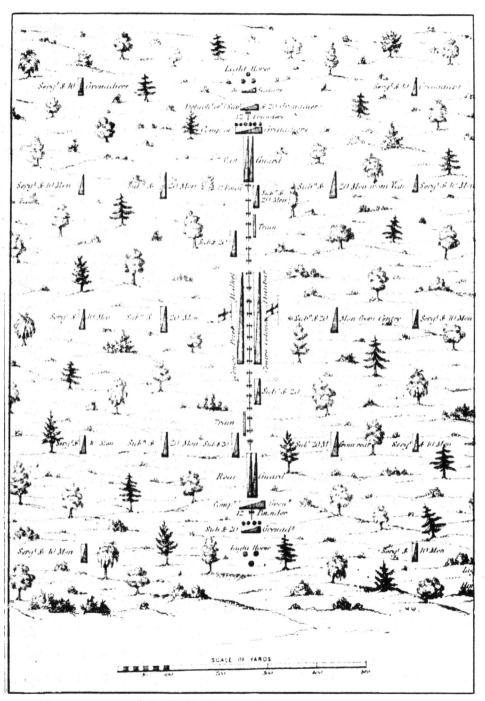

The advance unit of Braddock's Army on the march to Fort Duquesne. From Sargeant, *History of an Expedition Against Fort Duquesne.*

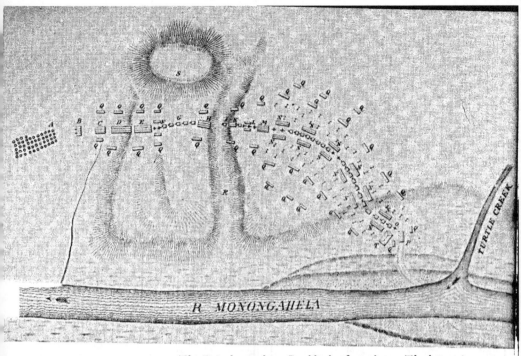

The French attack on Braddock—first phase. The letter A represents the French column before the attack; B, C, D, E, Q, etc., are units of Braddock's force on the march. Drawn by Pat Mackellar, Engineer of the Army. From Parkman, *Montcalm and Wolfe.*

The French attack on Braddock—final phase. The letter A shows the French and Indians surrounding the British; C, D, E, L, M, S show the front and rear of Braddock's force joined.

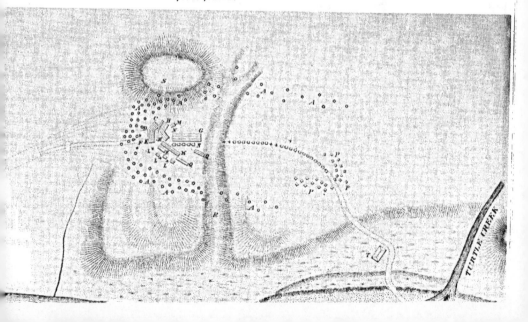

Braddock's defeat.   Painting by Edward Willard Deming.   Courtesy the State Historical Society of Wisconsin.

Braddock's grave.

Trace of the Braddock Road.

Post ends of the original stockade of Fort Necessity.

by the French, erosion of the surface, and other disturbances of the soil made this a difficult task, and led to varying ideas concerning the original structure. Much of the source material relating to the fort was not available to those who undertook early surveys and excavations. Only in recent years have research studies produced documentary evidence bearing on the shape and size of the stockade and defenses. This evidence, forming the basis of archeological investigation early in 1953, led to the definite establishment of the stockade location and the outlines of the entrenchments built by Washington's men.

Maps of the period were generally diagrammatic and contained only fragmentary evidence. Although certain charts indicated the fort as a small square, the repetition of the same, or similar, symbols for many fort locations implies that this was a conventional sign for a fortification and was not intended to indicate actual fort lines. Therefore, investigators turned early to ground evidence in an effort to establish the fort entrenchments and the stockade.

Contemporary methods of stockade construction, particularly those at Fort Le Boeuf and at Wills Creek, were well known to Washington. In the earlier attempts to locate the outlines of the fort, it was apparently assumed that the structure at Fort Necessity followed the general lines of contemporary forts with which Washington was acquainted.

The first known study of the ground surface was made by Freeman Lewis, a local surveyor, in 1816. In his attempt to locate the fort, he found clearly defined mounds, but the outlines were not sufficiently distinct to establish the original works. He concluded, on the basis of an examination of the 3-foot-high embankments on the southwest and southeast of Great Meadows Run, that the fort was triangular in shape. The existing mound led him to believe that the long side of the triangular fort was parallel to the stream bed and that a sector was projected to the creek to include a water supply within the fort bounds.

Jared Sparks, historian and traveler, visited the site in 1830. Observing closely the remnants of the embankments, Sparks concluded that the fort had four sides of nearly equal length, each approximately 35 yards long. For the clarification of his findings, Sparks prepared a sketch embodying his conclusions. Entrances were indicated on the southwest side, the direction from which the initial French attack developed. A supply of water being vital to occupants of the fort, Sparks indicated a bulge of the northeast corner to include the stream bed.

Seventy years passed before another effort was made to determine the appearance of the fort. In 1901, Robert McCracken, a civil engineer, made the first archeological approach to the problem. Aided by the findings of the Lewis survey and supplemented by his own study and excavations, McCracken believed the fort had four nearly equal sides and a projection to include the stream bed. Excavations undertaken near the creek unearthed a quantity of oak bark, believed to be remnants of the logs used in the original fort destroyed by the French. It was believed that the stockade had been implanted on the line of the entrenchments.

Additional excavation work was undertaken in 1931 by Harry R. Blackford, also a civil engineer. Conducting further digging in the mounds near the stream bed, Blackford located remnants of the original palisade 3 feet below the surface near the northern and northeastern embankments and adjacent to the stream. The post ends varied considerably in thickness and the tops showed signs of having been exposed to the action of time and water. At various points in this area, according to Blackford, "pieces of charred wood and lumps of charcoal were excavated from a depth of about three feet, this giving evidence to support the statement that the stockade was burned." He concluded that the original stockade had been built on the entrenchments, the outlines of which could readily be followed. Therefore, the reconstructed stockade built in 1932 was placed upon the line of the restored entrenchments.

Discovery of the Original Fort

Faced with the problem of replacing posts, many of which had become badly deteriorated since the erection of the stockade in 1932, the National Park Service, in 1952, first made a restudy of all available records bearing on the location and shape of the original fort and trenches. Then, a thorough archeological analysis of ground evidence was made, the results of which might establish definitely the type of fort and the kind, as well as the location, of trenches constructed by Washington's force in 1754.

While it could be reasonably concluded, on the basis of Washington's several references to the fort and stockade during the process of construction, that the enclosure was small and could be defended from entrenchments built near it, two documents lend particular weight to the hypothesis that the stockade was small and round in shape. In 1952, a deposition by John B. W. Shaw, who saw action at Fort Necessity, was discovered. Shaw, a member of the Virginia regiment, described first the actual fighting and then gave a realistic picture of the fort as a defense position. "There was at this Place," he relates, "a Small Stocado Fort made in a Circular form round a Small House that Stood in the Middle of it to keep our Provisions and Ammunition in, And was cover'd with Bark and some Skins, and might be about four-

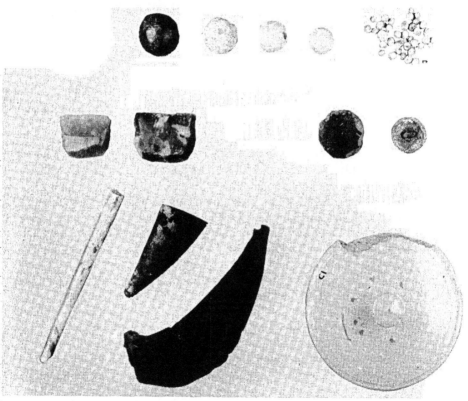

Relics of the Fort Necessity Battle.

Excavated trench showing post ends in place.

Mount Washington Tavern.

teen feet Square, and the Walls of the Fort might be eight feet Distance
from the said House all Round." Shaw's description of the action at
Fort Necessity ties in closely with Washington's account.

Shaw's statement concerning the fort, which apparently was based
on reasonably close examination, is supported by the observation of
Col. James Burd 5 years later. In 1759, Colonel Burd, in charge of
a road-clearing force of 200 men, preparing to open a new road from
Chestnut Ridge to Redstone, noted in his diary of September 10, as he
passed Fort Necessity, that he "Saw Col. Washington's fort, which
was called Fort Necessity. It is a small circular stockade, with a
small house in the center; on the outside there is a small ditch goes
around it about 8 yards from the stockade. It is situate in a narrow
part of the meadows commanded by three points of woods. There
is a small run of water just by it." In view of the reference by Colonel
Burd in 1759 to "a small circular stockade," it is possible that Burd
based his statement partly on his observation of the existing mounds
and partly on hearsay from settlers who had seen the stockade. It is
of importance to note, however, that certain observations made by
Burd corroborate the testimony of the eyewitness, John Shaw, contained in his deposition a few months after the battle.

On the basis of documentary evidence and previous explorations of
the mounds, the National Park Service in the summer of 1952 made
additional excavations to locate the "outer trenches" to which the
Washington and Shaw accounts referred. After careful examination

of the 1932 fill and earlier layers of soil, no evidence was found indicating that the trenches occupied by the South Carolina troops lay beyond the mounds of the existing fort outlines. Trenches were dug also on the interior of the stockade which, beyond indicating the original grade to be from 8 to 12 inches below the 1932 fill, disproved the existence of the long side of a triangular fort as advanced by the Lewis survey of 1816.

On the premise that the original fort was a small circular stockade, as indicated by the statements of John Shaw and Colonel Burd, and that the stockade constructed in 1932 was located approximately on the line of the original entrenchments, further excavation was undertaken during the spring and summer of 1953. As Burd had referred to a stream near the stockade and since pieces of the stockade had been discovered in the excavations of 1901 and 1932 near the stream in the northern area of the existing stockade, trenches were sunk in this area at an angle which would bisect a circle approximately 52 feet in diameter.

On the first day of excavating, the 3-foot-deep trench on the western perimeter of the hypothetical line revealed a large piece of wood, identified as one of the posts of the original stockade. The extension of the trench to the southern perimeter revealed a line of post ends, approximately 2 feet below the 1754 ground level, in a circular position. The earth adjacent to the posts was clearly the back-fill of soil for the support of the posts after they had been placed in position. Excava-

Marker on the Old National Pike.

tion along the course of the original trench, which could be readily followed, was extended eastward, revealing additional post ends in a circular outline. As the project neared completion, a sufficient number of post stubs had been found in their original position to determine definitely the construction details of the fort. The stubs represented the portion or the posts that stood below the ground-water level and were preserved because they had been continuously wet.

Archeological discoveries proved conclusively that the original stockade was circular in shape, measuring 53 feet in diameter. The overall perimeter was 168 feet, and the entrance, located on the southwest sector of the stockade, was 3.5 feet wide.

With the shape and location of the original stockade established, exploratory trenches were dug across the presumed location of the original outer entrenchments. Clearly defined cross sections of the trench on the back, or inner, side of the earthworks were secured. Sufficient information was obtained, therefore, to make possible a faithful restoration of these defense mounds.

Artifacts discovered in the 1953 excavations were similar to those found in the explorations of 1901 and 1932. Of first importance in the more recent excavations were the preserved post ends. Other artifacts included numerous lead musket balls, mostly of French caliber (.69); gun flints; small iron balls; clay tobacco-pipe fragments; the brass tip of a sword scabbard; a large bolt, possibly belonging to the gate; and a brass button.

Although archeological evidence of a small house, known to have been situated near the center of the stockade, was not found, a small log structure typical of the period has been erected to complete the restoration.

Guide to the Area

This guide is planned to help you reach points of historical interest at Fort Necessity and immediate vicinity and learn of the principal events which took place at each point.

1. FORT NECESSITY NATIONAL BATTLEFIELD SITE. Fort Necessity National Battlefield Site is administered by the National Park Service, United States Department of the Interior. Two acres in extent, it is entirely surrounded by Fort Necessity State Park, a 311-acre recreational area including the 234½-acre tract purchased by George Washington in 1769 and owned by him until the time of his death.

As you approach the fort by the footpath you will cross a small stream known as Indian Run. The junction of this stream and Great Meadows Run, to your right, was the location of the natural entrenchments to which Washington refers in one of his communications. Soon after the initial fortifications were completed, the circular stockade and small house on the interior were built for the safekeeping of supplies and ammunition. The present stockade was constructed in the spring of 1954 of split logs of irregular length and shape. The palisades are in the exact location of the original stockade posts which formed a circle 53 feet in diameter. The gate to the stockade is in the southwest sector of the circle.

The embankments in the foreground are authentic restorations of those built by Washington's men as defense positions during the brief time between the return of the men to the fort on July 1 and the beginning of the French attack on the morning of July 3. The French approached from the hillside on your left (then a wooded area), then shifted eastward to the fringe of trees on the southeast (back of you), from the cover of which the French and Indians directed much of their fire at the English force in the fort.

2. BRADDOCK ROAD. First blazed for the Ohio Company about 1750 by Nemacolin, a Delaware Indian, working with Thomas Cresap, a noted frontiersman, this road was improved and used by Washington in the Fort Necessity campaign in 1754 and by Braddock the following year. Extending from Wills Creek (Cumberland, Md.) to the Monongahela River, the road subsequently became a highway of westward expansion. At various times in its history this avenue of travel was known as Nemacolin's Path, Gist's Trail, Washington's Road, and Braddock Road. By 1817, when the National Road had been completed as far as the Monongahela River, the Braddock Road was abandoned. Only traces of the road bed, such as this section in a woodland area where the ground has not been disturbed, are still in evidence.

3. THE OLD NATIONAL PIKE. The road which replaced Braddock Road, variously known as the Old National Pike, the National Road, and the Cumberland Road, was the first step in the development of a national highway system. Conceived first in the mind of Washington, and later heartily advanced by Albert Gallatin and Henry Clay, the undertaking was given further impetus by the admission of Ohio into the Union in 1803. Three years later, Congress authorized the construction of a road from Cumberland, Md., to the State of Ohio, although actual construction did not begin until 1811.

The road commissioners pointed out in their report of 1808 that because of the "crooked and hilly course of the road [Braddock's] now traveled, the new route could not be made to occupy any part of it except an intersection on Wills Mountain, another at Jess Tomlinson's [Little Meadows], and a third near Big Youghioghana [Great

Schedule of rates on the Addison
Toll House.

Toll House at Addison, Pa., on the Old National Pike.

Crossings], embracing not a mile of distance in the whole without unnecessary sacrifices of distance and expense." The National Road followed generally the line of Braddock Road westward as far as Braddock Park, where Braddock Road veered northwestwardly to Fort Pitt (formerly Fort Duquesne). The National Road was extended westward and by 1819 had reached Wheeling, W. Va., where, due to prevailing economic conditions, work was suspended. In later years, construction of the road continued through Ohio and Indiana to central Illinois.

4. MOUNT WASHINGTON TAVERN. As the National Road was developed, many taverns were built along the route to serve as stopping places for stage coaches. In 1818, about the time that the National Road was opened to traffic through the Fort Necessity area, Judge Nathaniel Ewing of Fayette County, then owner of the Great Meadows tract, erected a large house beside the new road and named it Mount Washington. One of the first substantial buildings on the road between Little Meadows and Uniontown, it was operated by successive owners as a tavern, and because of its size and comfortable accommodations it was designated a stage house.

The Tavern, now used as a museum, is owned by the Commonwealth of Pennsylvania. Relics of the Fort Necessity and Braddock expeditions, many of which were found on the site of Fort Necessity and other historic areas in the vicinity, are on exhibit in the museum.

5. BRADDOCK'S GRAVE AND OLD ORCHARD CAMP. Old Orchard Camp, scene of Braddock's ninth encampment on June 25, 1755, during the expedition against Fort Duquesne, is located near the National Road, 1 mile west of Fort Necessity. On July 13, less than 3 weeks later, Braddock died and was buried here, at the first bivouac of the British troops in their panic-stricken retreat from the battlefield at Turtle Creek.

When Braddock Road was being repaired in 1804, workmen came upon a human skeleton in the middle of the road near the east bank of Braddock Run. With the bones were found buttons and buckles which indicated that the body had probably been clothed in a uniform of a British officer of rank. Believing that the remains were those of General Braddock, they were moved 100 yards southeast of the first grave and reinterred on a knoll which now overlooks the National Road.

In 1909, the citizens of Fayette County, Pa., organized the Braddock Park Association and acquired 23 acres of land, including a portion of the Old Orchard Camp site. Funds were raised for the erection of a monument, which was dedicated October 15, 1913. Held since 1931 by the Fort Necessity Chapter, Sons of the American Revolution,

Reconstructed Fort Necessity.

the area was transferred in 1952 to the Pennsylvania Department of Forests and Waters. The Braddock Road marker is located on the section of the road extending through Braddock Park.

6. HALF KING'S ROCKS. This massive rock formation, located on the crest of Chestnut Ridge, was the place where the Mingo Chief, the Half King, and Washington joined forces on the night of May 27, 1754, just before attacking the French force in a deep ravine 2 miles northward, since known as Jumonville Glen. Half King's Rocks, 1 mile north of U. S. 40, is located at a point where old Braddock Road joins the modern road.

7. JUMONVILLE GLEN. This secluded ravine, fringed on its western bank by a massive rock formation, was the scene of Washington's attack on Jumonville's small party of Frenchmen early on the morning of May 28, 1754. The reaction of the French at Fort Duquesne to this engagement brought about the Coulon de Villiers expedition of revenge against Washington which culminated in the action at Fort Necessity.

Located 3 miles north of U. S. 40, on the crest of Chestnut Ridge, the site was acquired and held for many years by the Fort Necessity Chapter, Sons of the American Revolution. In recent years, the site

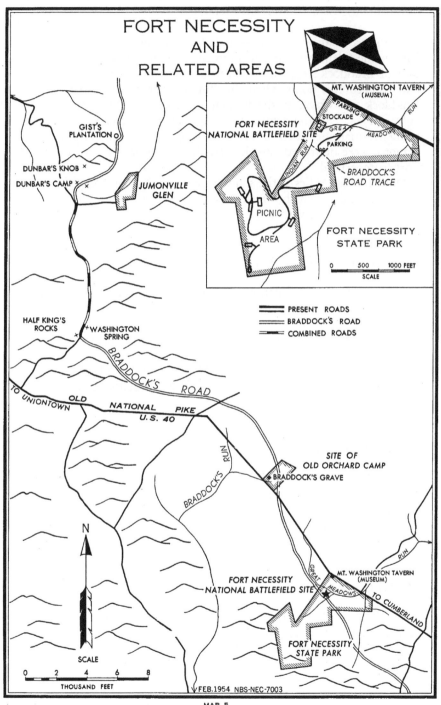

FORT NECESSITY
AND
RELATED AREAS

GIST'S
PLANTATION

DUNBAR'S KNOB ×
DUNBAR'S CAMP ×

JUMONVILLE
GLEN

Inset map:

MT. WASHINGTON TAVERN
(MUSEUM)

FORT NECESSITY
NATIONAL BATTLEFIELD SITE

STOCKADE
PARKING
GREAT
MEADOWS
PARKING
INDIAN RUN
RUN

BRADDOCK'S
ROAD TRACE

PICNIC

AREA

FORT NECESSITY
STATE PARK

0   500   1000 FEET
SCALE

HALF KING'S
ROCKS

× +WASHINGTON
SPRING

BRADDOCK'S   ROAD

━━━━ PRESENT ROADS
──── BRADDOCK'S ROAD
══ COMBINED ROADS

TO UNIONTOWN

OLD   NATIONAL   PIKE
U.S. 40

BRADDOCK'S RUN

SITE OF
OLD ORCHARD CAMP

✦ BRADDOCK'S GRAVE

N

FORT NECESSITY
NATIONAL BATTLEFIELD SITE

MT. WASHINGTON TAVERN
(MUSEUM)

GREAT
MEADOWS
RUN

TO CUMBERLAND

FORT NECESSITY
STATE PARK

SCALE

0   2   4   6   8
THOUSAND FEET

√ FEB. 1954 NBS-NEC-7003

MAP 5

and adjacent land have been owned by the Methodist Center of Pittsburgh and used as a Youth Recreational Camp.

8. DUNBAR'S CAMP. This site, situated a few hundred yards north of Jumonville Glen, was the encampment of Dunbar's regiment. This unit of Braddock's expedition, bearing the heavy arms and supplies, had reached this point when the ill-fated advance regiment led by Braddock was struck by the French and Indians at Turtle Creek on July 9, 1755. As the remnants from that field reached this camp, immense quantities of ammunition and supplies, as well as cannon and wagons, were destroyed, and Dunbar began a hurried retreat toward Fort Cumberland.

Dunbar's Camp lies at the southern base of Dunbar's Knob, a lofty, treeless eminence which offers, on a clear day, a magnificent view of the rolling country westward.

How to Reach Fort Necessity

Fort Necessity National Battlefield Site, located 11 miles east of Uniontown, Pa., may be reached over U. S. 40 from the west and east; from the Somerset interchange of the Pennsylvania Turnpike over State Route 53 to U. S. 40; from the Donegal interchange of the Turnpike over State Route 381 to U. S. 40; from Morgantown, W. Va., over U. S. 119 to U. S. 40 at Uniontown. U. S. 51 is a direct highway from Pittsburgh to U. S. 40 at Uniontown. Blue Ridge Bus Lines operate over U. S. 40.

About Your Visit

Information and free literature concerning the site may be obtained at the stockade. The services of the superintendent are available at the fort daily from 9 a. m. to 5 p. m. During the summer months, a ranger historian is also on duty.

Parking facilities are available a short distance from the fort.

Administration

Fort Necessity National Battlefield Site was acquired by the War Department in 1931 and transferred to the National Park Service in 1933. It is under the immediate supervision of the superintendent. Communications regarding the site should be addressed to the Superintendent, Fort Necessity National Battlefield Site, Farmington, Pa.

U. S. GOVERNMENT PRINTING OFFICE 1956   O—388186

NATIONAL PARK SERVICE

HISTORICAL HANDBOOK SERIES

FOR SALE BY THE SUPERINTENDENT OF DOCUMENTS, U. S. GOVERNMENT
PRINTING OFFICE, WASHINGTON 25, D. C.

Bandelier (No. 23), 35 cents

Custer Battlefield (No. 1), 20 cents

Custis-Lee Mansion (No. 6), 20 cents

Fort Laramie (No. 20), 25 cents

Fort McHenry (No. 5), 25 cents

Fort Necessity (No. 19), 25 cents

Fort Pulaski (No. 18), 25 cents

Fort Raleigh (No. 16), 20 cents

Fort Sumter (No. 12), 25 cents

Gettysburg (No. 9), 25 cents

Hopewell Village (No. 8), 25 cents

Independence (No. 17), 25 cents

Jamestown, Virginia (No. 2), 25 cents

Kings Mountain (No. 22), 25 cents

The Lincoln Museum and the House Where Lincoln Died
(No. 3), 20 cents

Manassas (Bull Run) (No. 15), 20 cents

Morristown, A Military Capital of the Revolution (No. 7),
25 cents

Petersburg Battlefields (No. 13), 30 cents

Saratoga (No. 4), 20 cents

Shiloh (No. 10), 25 cents

Statue of Liberty (No. 11), 25 cents

Vicksburg (No. 21), 25 cents

Yorktown (No. 14), 25 cents

and adjacent land have been owned by the Methodist Center of Pittsburgh and used as a Youth Recreational Camp.

8. DUNBAR'S CAMP. This site, situated a few hundred yards north of Jumonville Glen, was the encampment of Dunbar's regiment. This unit of Braddock's expedition, bearing the heavy arms and supplies, had reached this point when the ill-fated advance regiment led by Braddock was struck by the French and Indians at Turtle Creek on July 9, 1755. As the remnants from that field reached this camp, immense quantities of ammunition and supplies, as well as cannon and wagons, were destroyed, and Dunbar began a hurried retreat toward Fort Cumberland.

Dunbar's Camp lies at the southern base of Dunbar's Knob, a lofty, treeless eminence which offers, on a clear day, a magnificent view of the rolling country westward.

How to Reach Fort Necessity

Fort Necessity National Battlefield Site, located 11 miles east of Uniontown, Pa., may be reached over U. S. 40 from the west and east; from the Somerset interchange of the Pennsylvania Turnpike over State Route 53 to U. S. 40; from the Donegal interchange of the Turnpike over State Route 381 to U. S. 40; from Morgantown, W. Va., over U. S. 119 to U. S. 40 at Uniontown. U. S. 51 is a direct highway from Pittsburgh to U. S. 40 at Uniontown. Blue Ridge Bus Lines operate over U. S. 40.

About Your Visit

Information and free literature concerning the site may be obtained at the stockade. The services of the superintendent are available at the fort daily from 9 a. m. to 5 p. m. During the summer months, a ranger historian is also on duty.

Parking facilities are available a short distance from the fort.

Administration

Fort Necessity National Battlefield Site was acquired by the War Department in 1931 and transferred to the National Park Service in 1933. It is under the immediate supervision of the superintendent. Communications regarding the site should be addressed to the Superintendent, Fort Necessity National Battlefield Site, Farmington, Pa.

U. S. GOVERNMENT PRINTING OFFICE : 1956   O—388186

SD - #0119 - 160924 - C0 - 229/152/3 - PB - 9780282425685 - Gloss Lamination